A Note to Parents & Teachers—

Welcome to I See Insects from Xist Publishing! These books are designed to inspire discovery and delight in the youngest readers. Each book features very simple sentences with visual cues to help beginners read their very first text.

You can help each child develop a lifetime love of reading right from the very start. Here are some ways to help a beginning reader get going:

 Read the book aloud as a first introduction

 Run your fingers below the words as you read each line

 Give the child the chance to finish the sentences or read repeating words while you read the rest.

 Encourage the child to read aloud every day!

Copyright © Xist Publishing 2022
First Edition
All Rights Reserved.
No portion of this book may be reproduced without express permission from the publisher.

Published proudly in the State of Texas, USA by Xist Publishing
www.xistpublishing.com
24200 Southwest Freeway Suite 402- 290 Rosenberg, TX 77471
All images licensed from Adobe Stock
First Edition

Saddle Stitch ISBN: 978-1-5324-2853-1
Perfect Bound ISBN: 978-1-5324-4159-2
Hardcover ISBN: 978-1-5324-3336-8
eISBN: 978-1-5324-2828-9

I See Insects

Aphid

written by **August Hoeft**

I see an aphid.

The aphid is green.

The aphid has two antennae.

The aphid eats leaves.

The aphid lives on plants.

I see an aphid.

Things to do next!

Write a Sentence

I see an _____.

Drawing

Make a drawing of your favorite insect.

Sharing

Talk to your classmates about your favorite picture in this book. Explain to them why you like it.

WORD LIST

an
antennae
aphid
eats
green
has
I
is

leaves
lives
on
plants
see
the
two